MAKING MASKS
FOR SCHOOL PLAYS

BARBARA SNOOK

MAKING MASKS
FOR SCHOOL PLAYS

Publishers PLAYS Inc *Boston*

Library of Congress Catalog Card Number 76–180545
ISBN 0–8238–0131–4

First American edition published
in 1972 by Plays Inc

Printed and bound in Great Britain

CONTENTS

ACKNOWLEDGMENT

My very grateful thanks are due to Mr Philip Berry, Senior Lecturer at Rose Bruford Training College of Speech and Drama, for generously giving his time to a most helpful discussion of the place of the mask in education; to Mr R Fidge, Headmaster of Footscray Junior Church of England School for allowing me to visit his school, and to Miss P Reed who showed me some of the masks the children had made; to the Librarian of the Horniman Museum; to Mrs W Ellis for her help in correcting and criticising a rather awkward manuscript; and to Thelma M Nye for taking care of all the final stages of production.

Eastbourne 1972   *BLS*

Terracotta mask   Sparta sixth century BC

INTRODUCTION

Masks have been used for hundreds of years to help us enter the imaginative world, to creat an illusion of majesty, mystery, comedy and tragedy, important in carnival and theatre and, with even greater significance, in primitive religion where contact with the supernatural is established through mime and ritual dance. Among the many countries where masks are found some of the more interesting, as works of art, occur in West and Central Africa, the South Pacific Islands, Alaskan Eskimo and American Indian territory of the Pacific Northwest, Tibet and Burma. Masks are still used in Thailand and Ceylon, in Indonesian Wayang plays, and in the Noh plays of Japan; in modern Greek interpretation of classical plays; for religious fiestas in Mexico and Bolivia, and throughout Andean South America; at Mardi Gras in New Orleans and carnival in Nice; for May Day, Guy Fawkes and Hallowe'en; and as part of the make-up for some TV programmes.

In Japan they were once used as metal face guards during battle, and in Italy to protect the face from twigs while hunting through woodland. Roman masks are more closely connected with a study of armour than mime. Portrait burial masks used in Egypt and Mycenean Greece and small pectorial masks worn as decoration are also interesting for the quality of their craftsmanship. Working materials throughout the world are inevitably diverse, from rough hewn chunks of wood to elaborate woven basketry or fibre covered with a myriad brilliant feathers. Cowrie shells, tortoise-shell, seeds, fur, human and horse-hair also have their place. Colour is important whether it be a sombre scheme on a yard-long beak-snapping Kwakiutl raven, or a more sophisticated highly polished demon from Ceylon, gleaming with jewels set against a red, gold, black and white lacquered surface.

On primitive masks the arrangement of colour, generally limited to earth pigments, red, ochre, white, charcoal, grey and some blue,

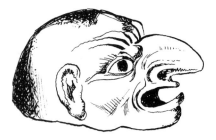

Clay mask   second century BC

exploits strong tone contrast aided by small areas of clearly defined pattern to emphasise dramatic effect, in a directness and simplicity which, if fully understood, can help to restrain our own much wider choice.

Colour may be an aid to identification and can help the audience to differentiate between formalised main characters and the minor characters designed with more natural, expressive faces; an imaginative approach can prevent a drama from being too realistic. It would, for example, be possible to mask the trolls in *Peer Gynt* and the devils in Glück's *Orpheus*, or in a simple fairy story to give the king and queen gold and silver masks.

In study sequence a museum visit may well result in bringing together an inspired selection of unusual materials for exploratory mask making; this would be followed by, or coincident with, writing a play for which serviceable, compared with purely decorative masks, are made. There is little justification for attempting to copy tribal masks other than as an exercise in the use of different media.

Some masks are temporary, easily discarded and destructible, made strong enough to last only for a brief performance. A folded piece of paper will then give more pleasure than an elaborate mask which has taken hours to make.

A mask must always be secure and comfortable to wear, speech must not be muffled nor vision impaired. If a child cannot see through a mask there is real danger and serious accidents have occurred as a result of blind movement. If mouth and eye holes are large in a full-face or hood mask, breathing is not hindered. Vision holes, if small, must be in exactly the right place. Hood masks can become heavy, hot and stuffy unless made large enough to fit loosely on the shoulders. Hat masks also can be heavy unless an effort is made to use light-weight material, but they do have the advantage of leaving the face completely uncovered.

Ancient Greek masks were over life size, with large eye and mouth openings. Similar to masks used in the Modern Greek Theatre's production of The Frogs

The mask will not only disguise and protect but also encourage the suppression of one personality and allow the wearer to assume another. While children make this transition to a new character instantaneously, adults may need time to grow into the part they wish to create.

In dramatic work with young children the mask has a valuable function, whether it be used for plays which have developed spontaneously, or for characters who help towards learning various skills, eg the postmaster or grocer in counting activity.

Relief comes to a shy child who, behind a mask, mimes freely and gains confidence to speak, believing himself unseen.

Stories woven round a group of characters in a market place or busy shopping street, a fairground or zoo, can bring together everyday events and extraordinary happenings, ordinary people and an element of fantasy. Legends from many lands dramatise successfully and short comedies akin to *Kyogen* from Japanese Noh plays, can be related to real life, adapted according to experience and student potentiality. Enactment of historical events, biblical stories, or incidents in the life of a different geographical region bring each its own pleasure in research and subsequent creation. At an older level some involvement in present day situations can be worked out in masked debate, taken beyond the mime of Kurt Jooss' famous ballet *The Green Table*. In complete contrast, true clowning makes light-hearted entertainment and a plea can be made for enough humour to alleviate horror and tragedy.

MATERIALS

Bric-a-brac   The following and similar items are useful:

Paper and plastic egg boxes   Polystyrene fruit trays   Cooking foil
and the sealing foil of large coffee tins   Frozen pie cases   One gallon
Gollicrush flagons   Breakfast cereal boxes   Drinking straws
Broken windscreen fragments   Large seed (sunflower, melon,
marrow)   Milk bottle tops   Lolly sticks   Dried grass   Straw
Hair   Fur   Brush bristles   Beads   Buttons   Curtain rings
Polo mints   Shells   Chopped straw   Sequin waste   Film strip
Old negatives   Scraps of coloured gelatine from stage lighting
Shoe-laces   Pipe cleaners   Sun goggles   Wood shavings   Paper
waste   Feathers   Table tennis balls cut in half for concave or
convex use   Corks   Macaroni   Rice   Lentils   Split peas
Pieces of pine cone

Adhesives

Copydex   Marvin Medium   Whygum   Evostick   Croid   Flour
paste   Glue pellets   Staples   Press-through paper clips with
prongs protected

Papers

Strong cartridge   Corrugated   Newsprint   Cellophane   Various
weight of cardboard   Crêpe paper   Coloured tissue   Paper bags
Doilies   Cream cartons   Cake cases   Sweet-box moulded linings

Other substances, fabrics and tools

Vaseline   Reinforcing rings   Starch   Rubber bands   Balloons
Vilene   Buckram   Muslin   Gauze   Net   Leather   Hessian   Poly-

styrene Bonded jersey Scissors Needles Scoring knife Razor
blade

Threads

Raffia Fibre string Teazed hemp Seagrass Various wires including fuse and florists's Fine elastic Hat elastic Flat metal
packing bands Cane Wool including mohair and various orna-
mental types

Paints

Designer's colours and gouache for more advanced work Tempera
block Polymer Ink Dye Felt pens Wax crayon Metallic
spray Varnish Glitter Plaster of paris Size Budgerigar sand

BALLOON MASKS

Masked heads on a glove puppet stage

A dressed mask
with some clothing
to hide shoulders

BUCKRAM

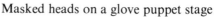

Oversew buckram with large
strong stitches, pulling
raw edges close together

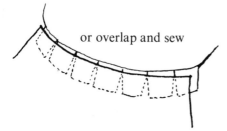

or overlap and sew

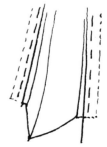

or inset and sew

Balloon method

Children working in pairs can take turns to hold steady the inflated balloon, or the tied end can be held to the table by a strip of adhesive tape. Have ready a small bowl of flour paste, some tissue paper and torn newspaper. Cover the balloon with vaseline or petroleum jelly to preserve it while work is in progress, for rubber is liable to perish. Smooth some large pieces of tissue paper over the vaseline to make a suitable surface for the rest of the work. Apply successive layers of paste and paper, with an occasional change of colour as a guide to thickness. A thin mask can be strengthened with a final cover of butter muslin, or it can be brushed over with size.

A second method, which has much to commend it, substitutes starch for flour paste. Cut tissue paper in long strips, dip them in starch, lay each strip on a board and roll the balloon along the paper which will adhere to it. Move the balloon's position slightly each time it is rolled, until evenly covered, and the papier mâché thick enough. This method is messy but enjoyable.

Pop the balloon and slice off the bottom of the mould making the large part fit the head. Add a rim for a hat, or decorate for character mask. When cut vertically the mould gives two equal pieces for full face masks.

Buckram on clay mould

Model the mask in clay; avoid very deep recesses. Allow it to dry hard. Cover the surface with a little vaseline. Damp the buckram and press firmly on to the mould using a blunt paint brush handle or modelling tool to help work the fabric into dips and creases. When set remove gently, without stretching the edges. Cut holes for eyes and mouth. Colour with a felt tipped pen rather than paint.

Squashed buckram

Make a trial mask with newspaper to find out how much buckram will be taken up when crumpled. The buckram must be damp but not sodden. It models easily by squashing and twisting, and its own stickiness makes it set firmly. Part of the mask may need to be tied with cotton to restrain it from spreading out again before the buckram has set. Large features such as nose or beak may be better modelled separately and sewn on afterwards with strong thread. A general tint of colour can be given while the fabric is still moist. Once the mask has set, colour should be as dry as possible when applied.

Cut and sewn buckram

Buckram can be sewn edge to edge with large deep stitches, or the edges snipped, overlapped and stab stitched together. Both methods may well be used on the same mask if an extra piece has to be set in a slit.

Card and paper

A paper mask is short-lived but often this does not matter and the results are all the more spontaneous from having been worked quickly. Any kind of paper sculpture, even of cartridge stout enough to allow score marks, is frail. Temporary masks made just for fun or for room decoration last longer if made of thin card into which lines can be scored with greater confidence.

Scoring requires a steady hand and should be practised on spare pieces of both paper and card until pressure and direction are controlled. Begin with straight lines folded into a zigzag before attempting to bend curves. Place the middle finger under the crease and bend the card away from the cut. A small-bladed penknife is preferable to a razor blade, being less pliable. Both paper and card will coil and twist if smoothed rapidly with a knitting needle or pencil. Good quality white card gives better results than straw-board which cracks raggedly. Card can be glued or stitched, folded, scored, modelled, and used as a support for metal foil. Reinforced with muslin it lasts for many performances. A little low-relief modelling may be added by means of cotton wool between muslin and card.

CARD AND PAPER MODELLING

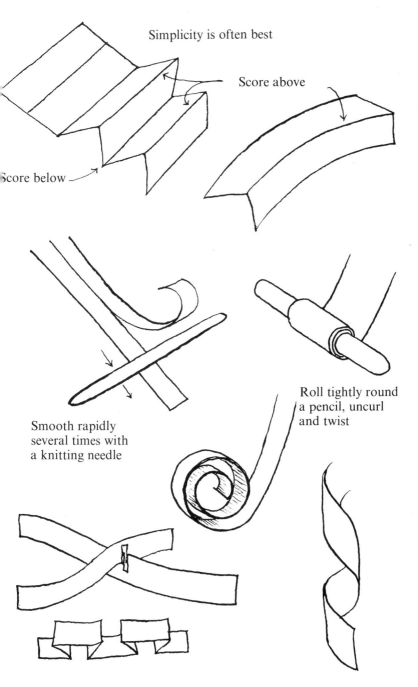

Simplicity is often best

Score above

Score below

Smooth rapidly
several times with
a knitting needle

Roll tightly round
a pencil, uncurl
and twist

CORRUGATED CARD

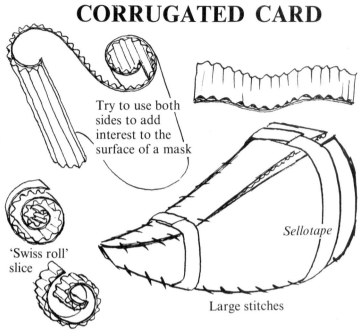

Try to use both sides to add interest to the surface of a mask

Sellotape

'Swiss roll' slice

Large stitches

Corrugated card

The natural colour of brown corrugated card can be put to good use, contrasting rough and smooth surfaces. On a flat mask, extra features, stuck along their edges, are less secure than if wedged into slits and glued with *Croid, Marvin Medium*, or similar adhesives. A wash of size strengthens the surface.

The pieces of a three dimensional mask should be neatly oversewn with straight deep stitches falling between the ridges. Selotape is reluctant to stick on the smooth side and will not do so over ridges but it holds pieces in place temporarily, if strapped right round and overlapped. A projecting mask with a basic construction of corrugated card needs oversewing with stitches 19 mm ($\frac{3}{4}$ in.) deep and about 25 mm (1 in.) apart. Further modelling with paste and paper covered by a layer of book muslin and a generous daubing all over with hot glue will, when set, make a very strong foundation for almost any type of decoration.

Vision holes should be cut before the application of glue. Stitch holes for a hood are made afterwards with a bradawl.

METAL FOIL

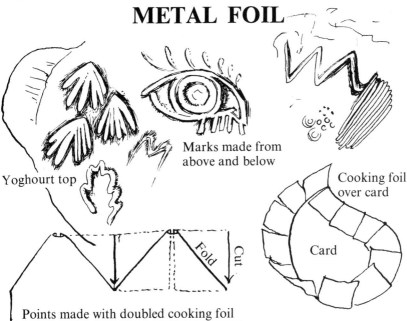

Yoghourt top

Marks made from
above and below

Cooking foil
over card

Card

Fold Cut

Points made with doubled cooking foil

Metal foil

There are several sources of metal foil. Useful pieces can be salvaged
from pre-packed meal containers, and pie cases; heavy foil used to
seal large tins of instant coffee is easily cut with scissors and modelled.
Yoghurt tops, not quite as thick, serve well for smaller decoration;
they emboss excellently.

Ordinary cooking foil crumples directly it is handled. It can be
smoothed over card and burnished back to shininess by rubbing in
a circular movement with a finger nail. Lines drawn with a blunt
point into this surface make good texture areas but show less from
a distance than might be expected. Stronger results come from
modelling over string previously glued to the foundation card.
Cooking foil, doubled, will only just stand alone; single thicknesses
need glueing to card or paper. A folded edge should be used with
great care.

Papier mâché

Papier mâché is made from a combination of paper fragments and stiff flour paste. A very hard form can be made from a mixture of paper, glue powder, sawdust and plaster of paris; this is very hard indeed and much easier to prepare than fibre glass.

Balloon masks are covered with papier mâché made with strips of paper. Cardboard masks can be slightly modelled with papier mâché if care is taken to choose a card thick enough not to be distorted by the pull of the paste.

When papier mâché covers a clay or plasticine head the modelling should be emphasised because each layer of paper will tend to smooth out the features. Work on a clean surface; allow the clay to dry out slowly, to prevent cracks. Cover with a layer of vaseline, followed by successive layers of paste and paper until the mask is about 3 mm ($\frac{1}{8}$ in.) thick. When perfectly dry, ease gently off the base. Clear away particles lodged in nose or chin, and if necessary plug with a little more papier mâché for strength. Bore holes with an awl for elastic, at ear level. Smooth down rough edges and protect with surgical tape. Cut vision holes and a space for the mouth. Although a papier mâché mask takes a long time to make, the result is rewarding because the firm substance forms such an excellent base for further decoration.

PAPIER MÂCHÉ

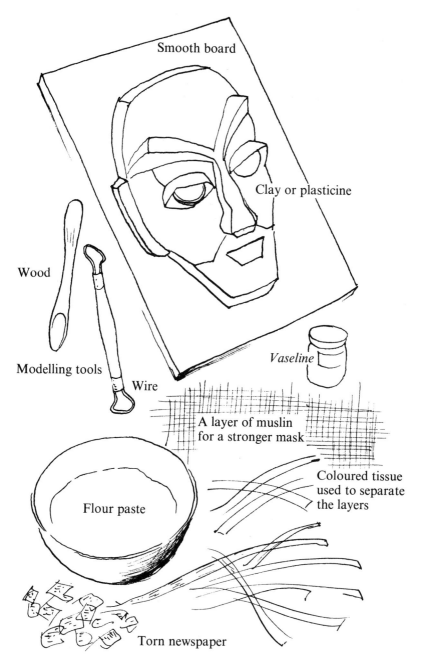

Smooth board

Clay or plasticine

Wood

Modelling tools

Wire

Vaseline

A layer of muslin
for a stronger mask

Coloured tissue
used to separate
the layers

Flour paste

Torn newspaper

PLAITED STRAW

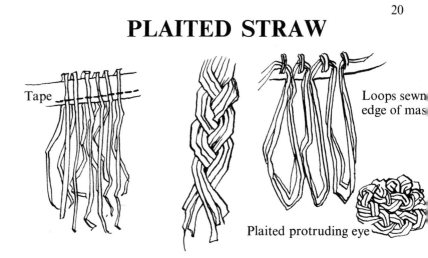

Tape

Loops sewn
edge of mas

Plaited protruding eye

Plaited straw

Straw, dried grass and raffia are more useful for detail than for whole masks which easily grow cumbersome. Their texture has an affinity with hessian which, either stiffened with size or mounted over card, makes a suitable background material. (The wide colour range now available has transformed this rather ordinary fabric into a stimulating ground for subtle or strong colour schemes). Straw should be soaked until it is soft enough to be worked without cracking. The pleasant golden sheen, round hard stems and flat blades contrast well with the natural grey-green shades and pale yellows of dried grass. A grass plait can be strengthened by incorporating string, leading stems of vine, creeper, or honeysuckle so strong that they need cutting with a knife.

Coiled plaits should be sewn to shape, then either assembled as a whole mask or glued where needed for special decoration on to a background. Vision holes below a protruding straw eye can be disguised with pattern.

Several layers of straw, raffia or garden bast, knotted over stout string or folded over tape and sewn, will make impressive beards or manes.

Many African masks are surrounded with holes which show where fibre manes once were attached.

Plaster of paris

Plaster of paris sets rapidly therefore work must be planned carefully and done quickly. Sprinkle plaster through a sieve evenly on to a bowl of water, until level with the water. Stir carefully but do not let in any air bubbles. Use immediately, work fast and endeavour to complete the task before the plaster sets. Do not mix more than necessary. It is better to under estimate rather than have too much. A second mixture will adhere to the first if this has been left rough. NB Use a washing up bowl for cleaning and do not let any plaster escape into the sink. Drain sediment on to paper and put in the dustbin.

Wood shavings or paper waste mixed into wet plaster of paris give an unusual texture; straws may be used whole or chopped and feathers too can be embedded or stuck in by their quills. Plaster can be coloured with tempera paint, dye or ink. Large areas of colour are difficult to manage because plaster is very absorbent and paint tends to soak in unevenly. Small areas of colour generally look more compelling and dramatic.

Polystyrene

Polystyrene is an interesting material to work with although messy, because tiny foam fragments are so light that they blow all over the place and cling to everything. Tiles can be cut with a Proop's polystyrene foam cutter which is used like a fretsaw, or cut painstakingly with a razor blade.

Foam pieces must be stuck together with an adhesive which does not eat holes through the tile.

Tiles cannot be bent. They can be excavated to different levels, ornamented with coloured cellophane and the surface can be built out with successive layers of tile. A method has to be devised to keep the mask away from the face. A stick mask is the obvious solution but the effect, when made into a hood mask, is far more exciting.

Paint and metallic sprays take well, and small objects can be embedded into the uneven surface. Thin polystyrene used for insulation, is flexible but at the same time tears and cracks very quickly. If used for mask construction it would have to be mounted on fabric with the special adhesive supplied for application to a wall.

VILENE

Vilene

The heaviest grade of *vilene* is strong enough to stand up to limited use. Two thicknesses machined together make a stout fabric. The surface takes paint, but in order to keep the softness which is the outstanding quality of colour on *vilene*, pigment should be fairly dry. *Freart* crayon, *Craypas*, and coloured ink drawn with a felt tipped pen, all give a slightly plush effect and are easier to control than paint. Ordinary lead pencil, B or 2B, takes well over all these methods but is insignificant alone. Since the material does not fray edges may be elaborately shaped. Withstand a temptation to use pinking shears which are mechanical and monotonous compared with freely cut, spontaneous zigzag lines.

THE DOMINO

The Birds
by Aristophanes

Greek National Theatre

The domino

Italian clowns first used the domino in the sixteenth century. The name 'masque' for a type of play, is related to this early use. By the eighteenth century the custom of covering the upper half of the face was well established for theatre and festivity. Venetian artists depicted men and women wearing dominos some of which were deep enough to cover the upper lip, others with a very elongated nose and moustache. A reveller wearing this disguise, with cloak and hood, would be completely unrecognisable.

The use of the domino has persisted. In the modern Greek theatre production of Aristophanes' *The Birds* dancers, in leotard style costumes, with feathered forearms, tails and headdressed, wear simple dominos which contribute greatly to the atmosphere of fantasy, and hinder neither dance nor song. Where the domino is moulded over the bridge of the nose the edge should be padded to prevent chafing. A little surgical plaster covers rough edges satisfactorily and is easily painted to match surrounding colour.

A comfortable domino can be made from bonded jersey, a foam-backed stretch fabric. When eye holes are cut, make allowance for the fact that the jersey will stretch over the face. The mask is held firmly in place with black ribbon.

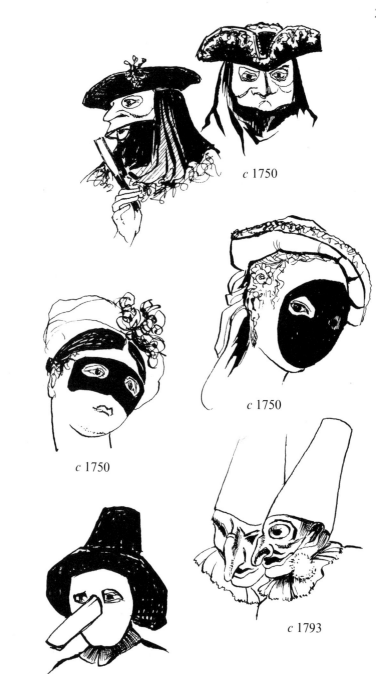

c 1750

c 1750

c 1750

c 1648

c 1793

Masks from Venetian paintings

DOMINO

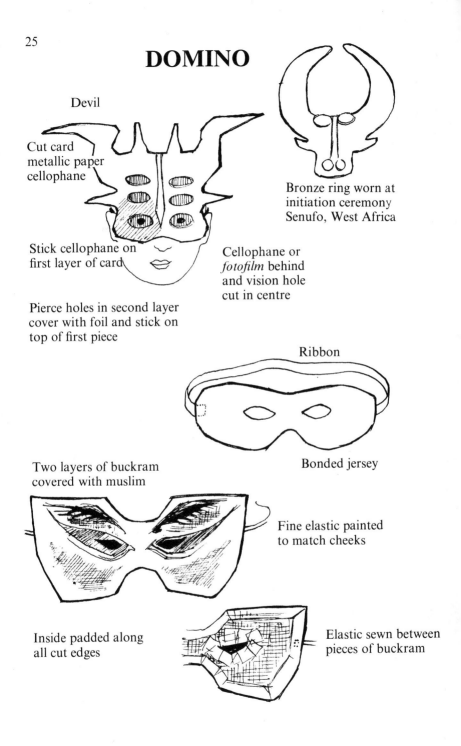

Devil

Cut card
metallic paper
cellophane

Stick cellophane on
first layer of card

Pierce holes in second layer
cover with foil and stick on
top of first piece

Cellophane or
fotofilm behind
and vision hole
cut in centre

Bronze ring worn at
initiation ceremony
Senufo, West Africa

Ribbon

Bonded jersey

Two layers of buckram
covered with muslin

Fine elastic painted
to match cheeks

Inside padded along
all cut edges

Elastic sewn between
pieces of buckram

Extended domino mask
of corrugated paper

Eskimo wooden mask

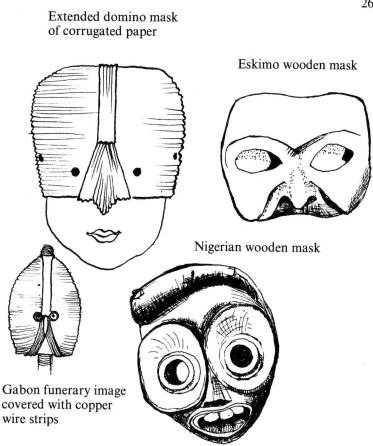

Nigerian wooden mask

Gabon funerary image
covered with copper
wire strips

Always allow room for the nose

Do not cut a hole for it to poke through

Either add a nose or curve the mask over
the bridge of the nose

When fitting the mask over the face to find
the position of the features, use a very soft
pencil and draw gently

Never cut with the mask in position

Extra string sometimes needed

Cream carton
or paper cut

Paper cone

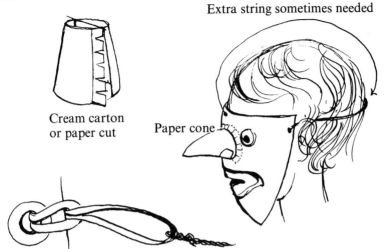

Looped rubber band and string

Pipe cleaners
worn over the ears

Plastic egg carton eyes

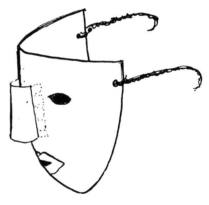

Hat elastic may not be
readily available for a
hastily made mask.
Improvise with a looped
rubber band through each
eyelet hole, and join with
string

A partly modelled half-mask

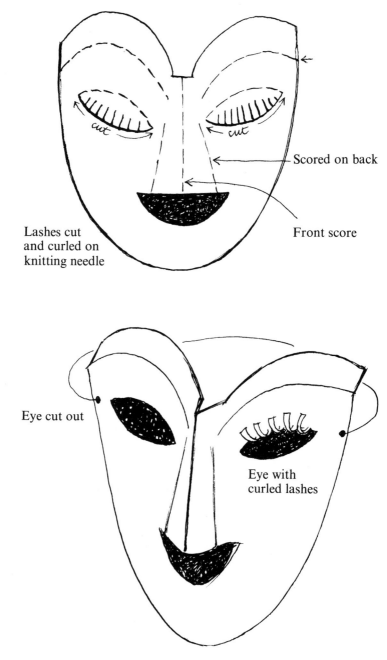

Scored on back

Front score

Lashes cut
and curled on
knitting needle

Eye cut out

Eye with
curled lashes

HALF-FACE MASKS

Cut paper wide enough to allow for folds

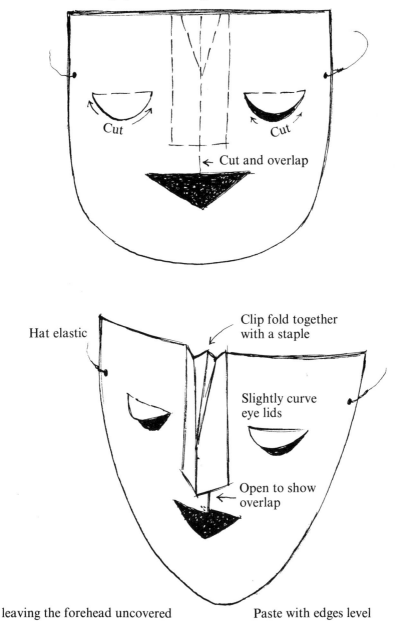

Cut

Cut

← Cut and overlap

Hat elastic

Clip fold together
with a staple

Slightly curve
eye lids

Open to show
overlap

leaving the forehead uncovered

Paste with edges level

Huge sun-glasses may in themselves mask sufficiently

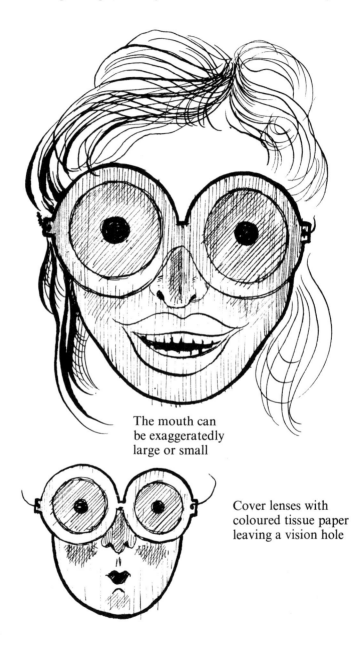

The mouth can
be exaggeratedly
large or small

Cover lenses with
coloured tissue paper
leaving a vision hole

STICK MASKS

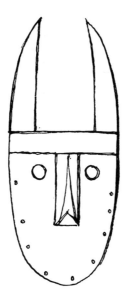

Toma flat wood

Stick masks

The stick mask presents no ventilation problem, there is nothing to muffle the voice and the actor can easily see where to move. The main disadvantage is that with one hand always occupied gesture is restricted to the other free hand. The mask should be large enough to overcome the temptation to peep round the edge, yet be of sensible proportion and fairly light. It must be held steadily, not waved about like a fan.

The supporting stick, which needs to be firmly secured, can be sandwiched between two masks, enabling the actor to take two parts. Double masks, though not stick masks, are used in several parts of the world.

Stick masks need not be flat. A fully shaped face mask can be attached to a stick if for any reason a normal mask is inconvenient. The upright stick should be made of dowelling or the thicker end of a garden cane; cross bars can be made from an old paint brush (hog) handle or thin garden cane.

Always test animal masks on a small scale with paper cut and *sellotaped* together. A slight change in position and size of ear and eye will quickly transform a basic mask from one animal into another. Indian beggars use stick masks made of painted fabrics; these are not intended to hide the face but to draw attention to the supplicant.

Brow line
changes in
expression

FATHER CHRISTMAS

GUY FAWKES

CHEF

FARMER, MARKET GARDENER

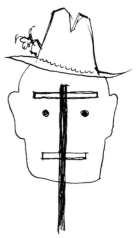

Back view

Paint on *vilene* pasted
on a card base, for a
plush effect

Stick held in place
by stapled strips of
card and gummed linen
tape

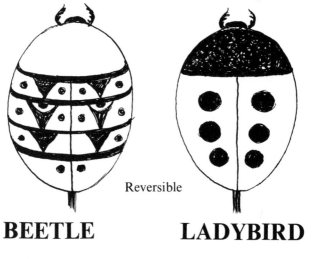

Reversible

BEETLE   LADYBIRD

Eye holes may be cut out but are not
essential on a stick mask because it
is held away from the face

BUTTERFLY

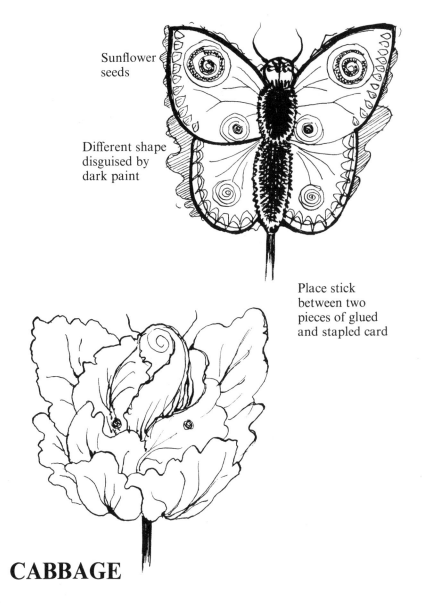

Sunflower
seeds

Different shape
disguised by
dark paint

Place stick
between two
pieces of glued
and stapled card

CABBAGE

A reversible mask enables
the actor to play two parts
in quick succession

BEAR

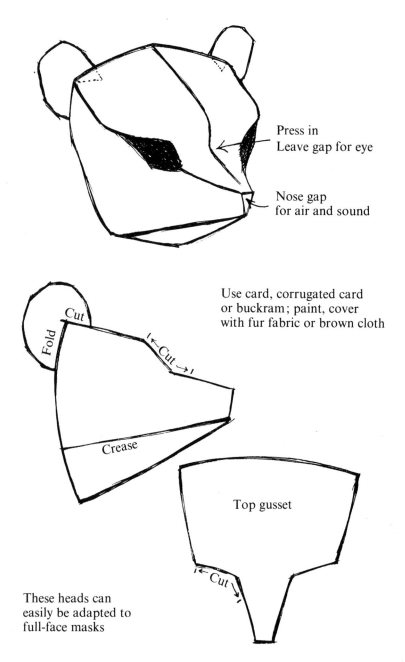

Press in
Leave gap for eye

Nose gap
for air and sound

Use card, corrugated card
or buckram; paint, cover
with fur fabric or brown cloth

Fold

Cut

Cut

Cut

Crease

Top gusset

Cut

These heads can
easily be adapted to
full-face masks

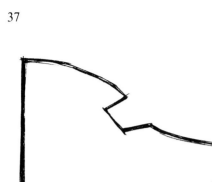

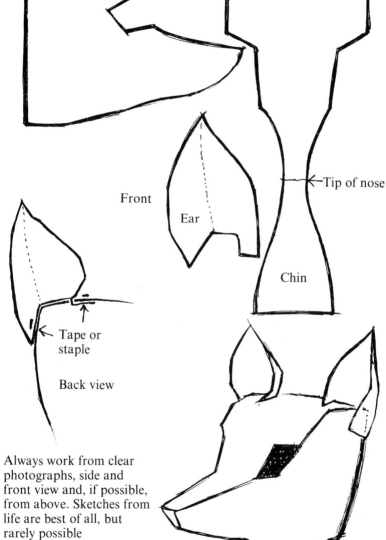

Cut for ear

Front

Ear

←Tip of nose

Chin

Tape or
staple

Back view

Always work from clear
photographs, side and
front view and, if possible,
from above. Sketches from
life are best of all, but
rarely possible

MOUSE

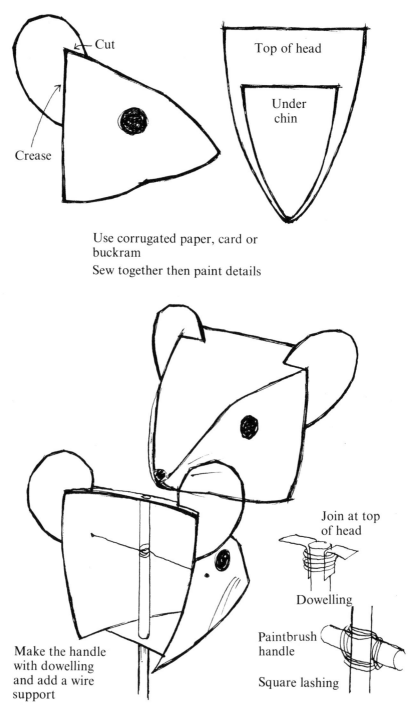

Cut

Crease

Top of head

Under chin

Use corrugated paper, card or buckram

Sew together then paint details

Join at top of head

Dowelling

Paintbrush handle

Square lashing

Make the handle with dowelling and add a wire support

GIRAFFE

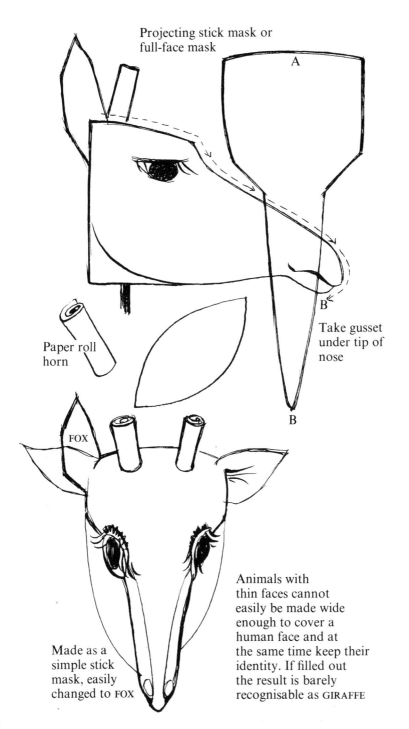

Projecting stick mask or full-face mask

A

Paper roll horn

Take gusset under tip of nose

B

B

FOX

Made as a simple stick mask, easily changed to FOX

Animals with thin faces cannot easily be made wide enough to cover a human face and at the same time keep their identity. If filled out the result is barely recognisable as GIRAFFE

DONKEY

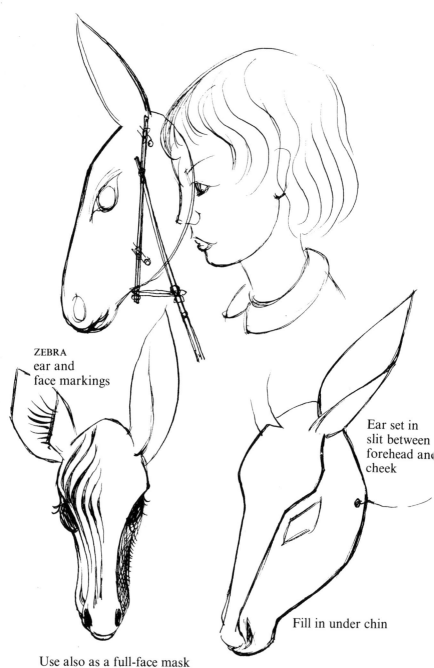

ZEBRA
ear and
face markings

Ear set in
slit between
forehead and
cheek

Fill in under chin

Use also as a full-face mask
tied at cheek

Small gap for tongue

WHOLE FACE

Iroquois twisted face

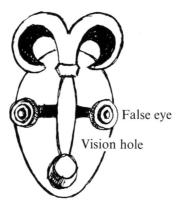

False eye

Vision hole

Ogoni-wood
eyes beyond vision holes

The full face mask gives endless opportunity for the use of different media and there is a temptation here to experiment for experiment's own sake. While plenty of amusement can be gained from creating curious faces, this is a doubtful end in itself. Masks can be used for room decoration but are of more value when related to dramatic production.

A study of primitive masks broadens the approach to shape and character identification, to variety of materials and conversely to colour limitation. On the stage deliberate irregularity in features, which in a native mask will have ritual significance, adds vigour to expression.

A rough paper mask should always be made as a preliminary, and on it the position of openings marked. Speech and vision will not be impaired if these are accurate. It is possible to see through a remarkably small hole if it is in the right place. The eye on the mask need not coincide with vision holes, and the mouth opening need not coincide with the painted mouth, if in both instances true openings are camouflaged. The nose projection must however be sufficiently in line for comfort, and have air holes.

The upside down face is an exception to this rule.

If the action of the play demands that a masked character shall eat or drink, an upper half-face domino or hat mask must be used. A mask which is held on by elastic fits closely, touching the skin in several places. The inside should be smooth, clips and staples covered with linen tape, rough edges of card or buckram covered with surgical plaster, and if necessary, on a mask which will have a fairly long life, lint pasted over the entire inner surface.

43

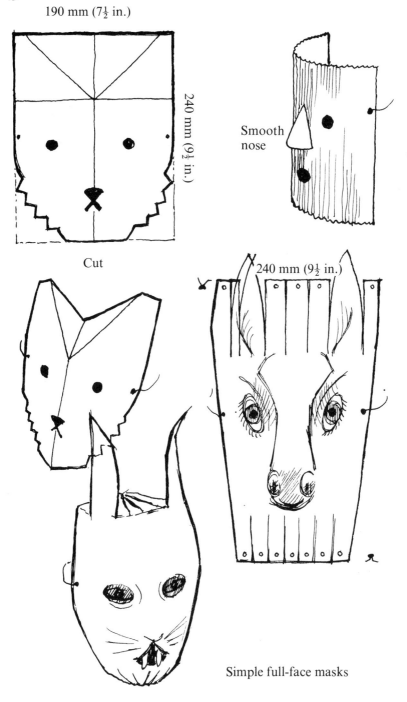

190 mm (7½ in.)

240 mm (9½ in.)

Cut

Smooth
nose

240 mm (9½ in.)

Simple full-face masks

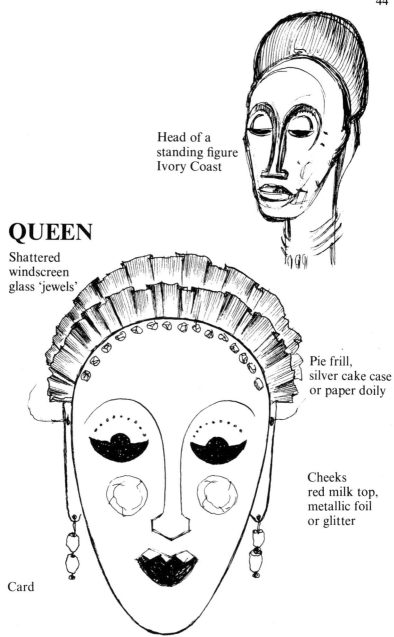

Head of a
standing figure
Ivory Coast

QUEEN

Shattered
windscreen
glass 'jewels'

Pie frill,
silver cake case
or paper doily

Cheeks
red milk top,
metallic foil
or glitter

Card

Cover entirely with cooking foil
or spray with metallic paint

ARISTOCRATS

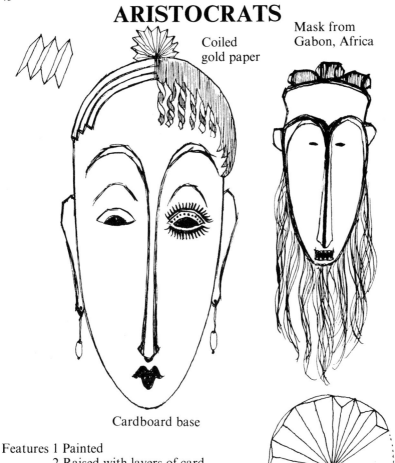

Coiled
gold paper

Mask from
Gabon, Africa

Cardboard base

Paper top-knot

Features 1 Painted
2 Raised with layers of card
3 Outlined with very thick wool

Try discarded false eyelashes instead of paint

Hair – scored or twisted paper

Thin *vilene* over cardboard takes colour excellently

CLOWN

Northern Torres Straits

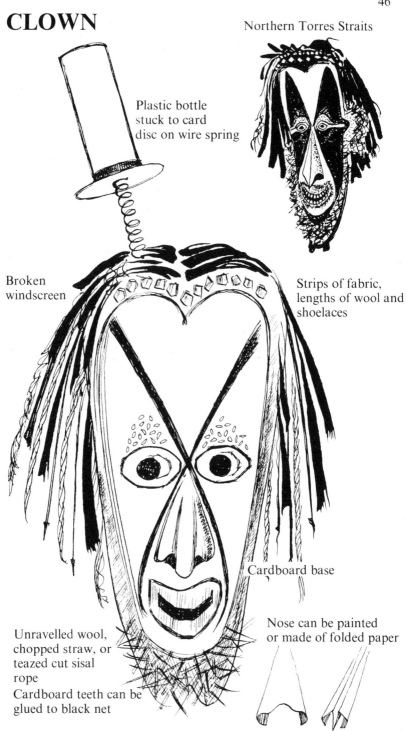

Plastic bottle
stuck to card
disc on wire spring

Broken
windscreen

Strips of fabric,
lengths of wool and
shoelaces

Cardboard base

Nose can be painted
or made of folded paper

Unravelled wool,
chopped straw, or
teazed cut sisal
rope
Cardboard teeth can be
glued to black net

TRAMP or BEGGAR

Use card covered with butter muslin or hessian
to provide a rough surface and to increase strength

Teazed rope, straw and raffia

Spot with lentils

From a Melanesian wooden mask, painted in pink,
blue, smoke-grey and white. Vegetable fibre and
dried leaves for hair and beard

◄ Circus clowns wear a mask-like make-up which is
more practical than a loose mask

DEITY
KING or QUEEN

From New Guinea

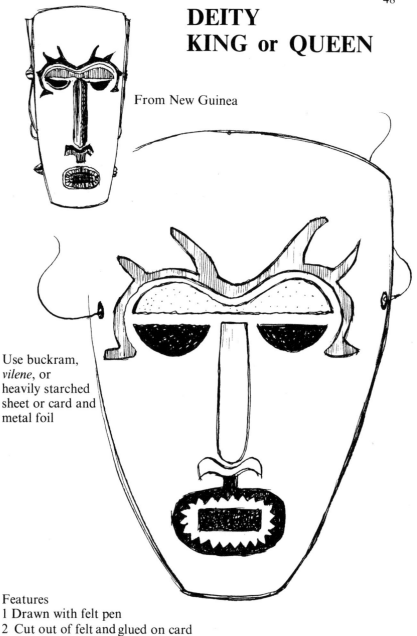

Use buckram,
vilene, or
heavily starched
sheet or card and
metal foil

Features
1 Drawn with felt pen
2 Cut out of felt and glued on card
3 Lines drawn with glue, and
   dusted over with budgerigar sand
4 Low relief, 4 to 6 layers of superimposed card

PRINCESS

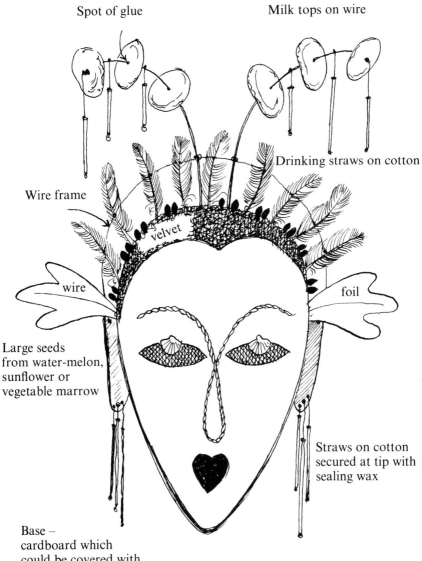

Spot of glue

Milk tops on wire

Drinking straws on cotton

Wire frame

velvet

wire

foil

Large seeds
from water-melon,
sunflower or
vegetable marrow

Straws on cotton
secured at tip with
sealing wax

Base –
cardboard which
could be covered with
vilene or metal foil

Shell eyes glued on to black net

WARRIOR

based on Micronesian mask

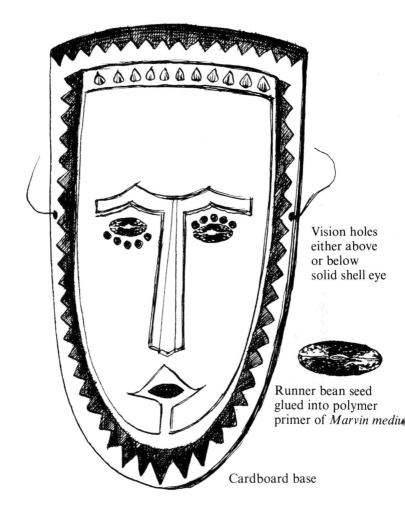

Vision holes
either above
or below
solid shell eye

Runner bean seed
glued into polymer
primer of *Marvin mediu*

Cardboard base

Eyebrows and nose raised with several layers of cardboard
Mouth painted
Cut and folded metal foil decoration (see page 17)
Design would adapt to polystyrene method with hood

WARRIOR

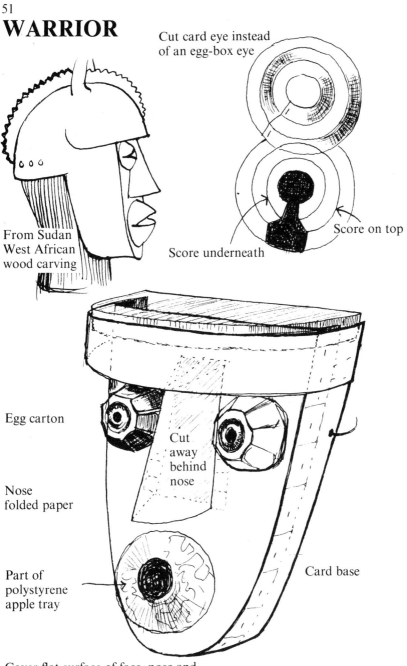

Cut card eye instead
of an egg-box eye

From Sudan
West African
wood carving

Score on top

Score underneath

Egg carton

Cut
away
behind
nose

Nose
folded paper

Part of
polystyrene
apple tray

Card base

Cover flat surface of face, nose and
chin strap with cooking foil

UPSIDE-DOWN FACE

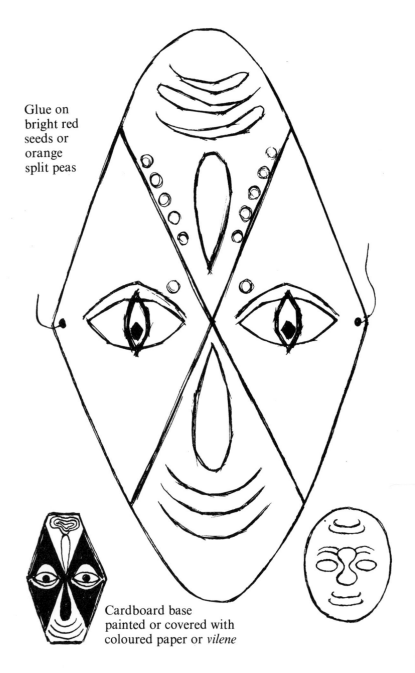

Glue on
bright red
seeds or
orange
split peas

Cardboard base
painted or covered with
coloured paper or *vilene*

53

UPSIDE-DOWN FACE

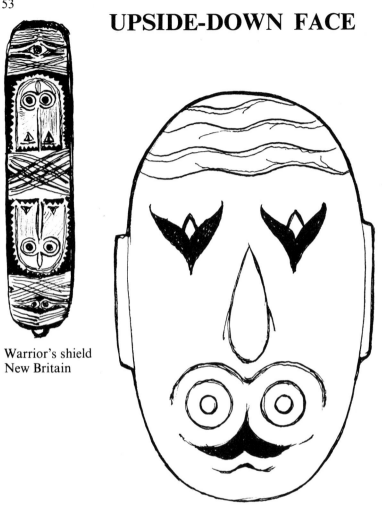

Warrior's shield
New Britain

Keep turning the mask up and down while it is
being drawn. Some liberties may have to be
taken with shapes
Cardboard or stiff paper, with paint

MAN and OWL

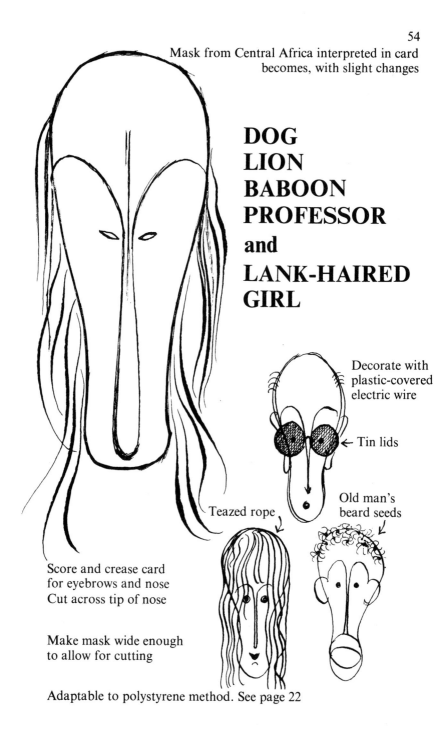

Mask from Central Africa interpreted in card
becomes, with slight changes

DOG
LION
BABOON
PROFESSOR
and
LANK-HAIRED
GIRL

Decorate with
plastic-covered
electric wire

← Tin lids

Old man's
beard seeds

Teazed rope

Score and crease card
for eyebrows and nose
Cut across tip of nose

Make mask wide enough
to allow for cutting

Adaptable to polystyrene method. See page 22

55

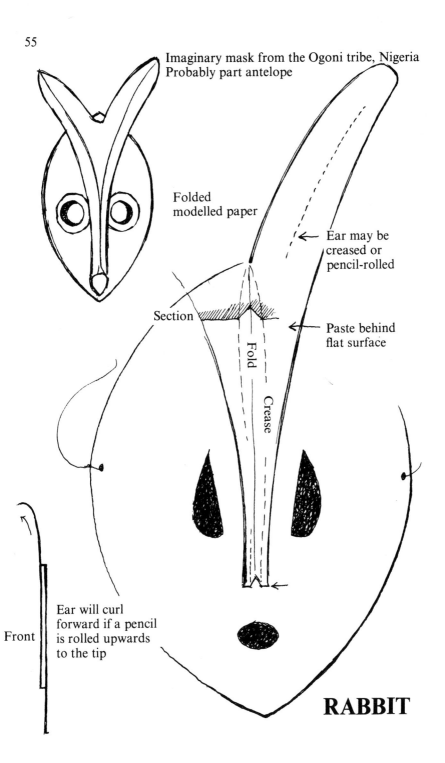

Imaginary mask from the Ogoni tribe, Nigeria
Probably part antelope

Folded
modelled paper

Ear may be
creased or
pencil-rolled

Paste behind
flat surface

Section

Fold

Crease

Ear will curl
forward if a pencil
is rolled upwards
to the tip

Front

RABBIT

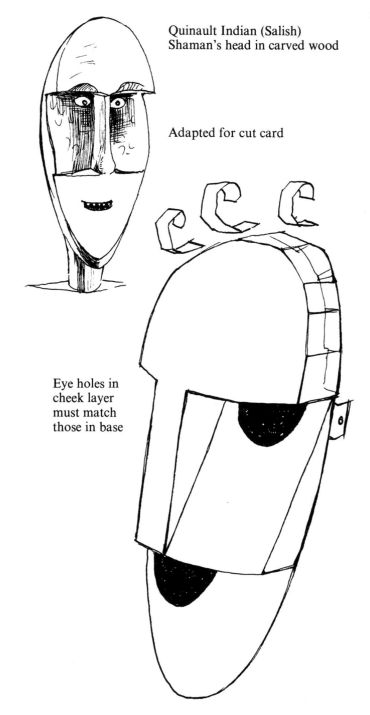

Quinault Indian (Salish)
Shaman's head in carved wood

Adapted for cut card

Eye holes in
cheek layer
must match
those in base

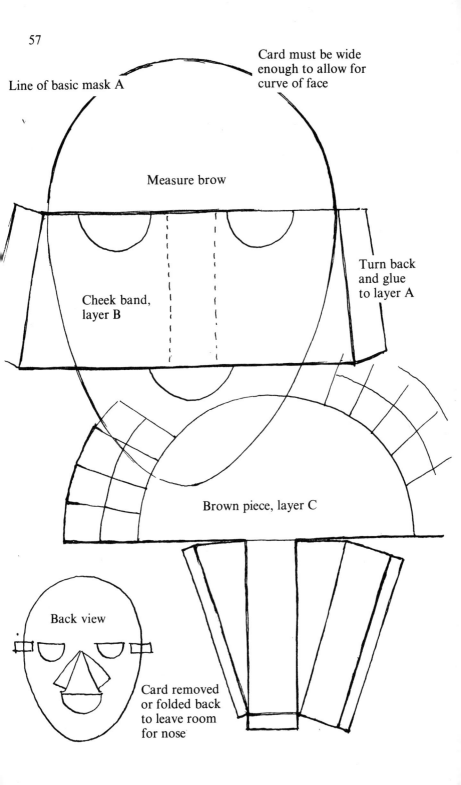

Line of basic mask A

Card must be wide
enough to allow for
curve of face

Measure brow

Cheek band,
layer B

Turn back
and glue
to layer A

Brown piece, layer C

Back view

Card removed
or folded back
to leave room
for nose

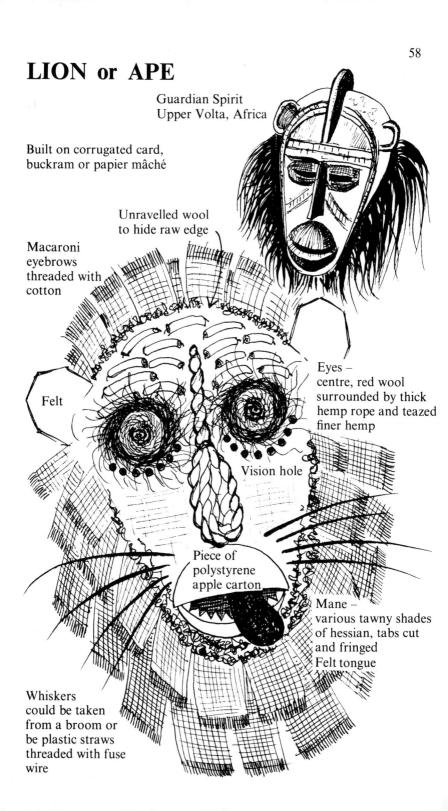

LION or APE

Guardian Spirit
Upper Volta, Africa

Built on corrugated card,
buckram or papier mâché

Unravelled wool
to hide raw edge

Macaroni
eyebrows
threaded with
cotton

Felt

Eyes –
centre, red wool
surrounded by thick
hemp rope and teazed
finer hemp

Vision hole

Piece of
polystyrene
apple carton

Mane –
various tawny shades
of hessian, tabs cut
and fringed
Felt tongue

Whiskers
could be taken
from a broom or
be plastic straws
threaded with fuse
wire

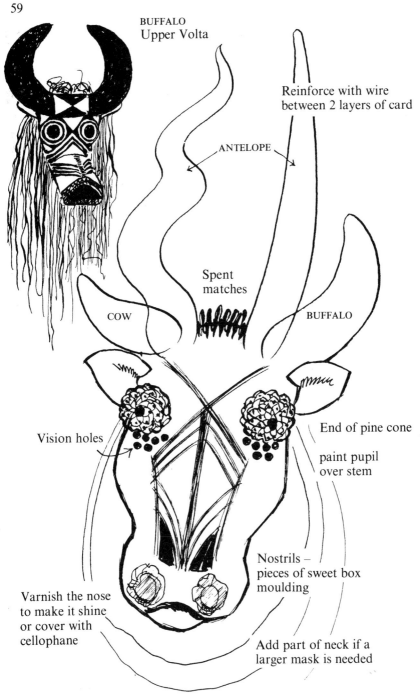

BUFFALO
Upper Volta

Reinforce with wire
between 2 layers of card

ANTELOPE

Spent
matches

COW

BUFFALO

End of pine cone

paint pupil
over stem

Vision holes

Nostrils –
pieces of sweet box
moulding

Varnish the nose
to make it shine
or cover with
cellophane

Add part of neck if a
larger mask is needed

Base of corrugated cardboard or buckram

ANIMAL FACES

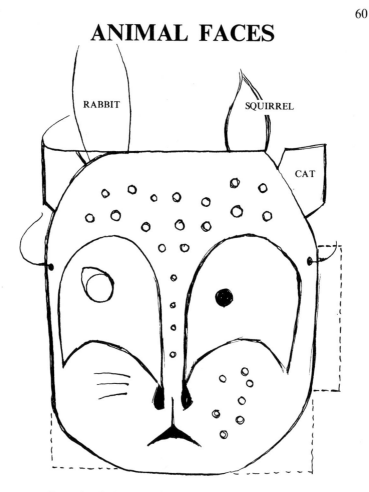

RABBIT

SQUIRREL

CAT

Paste back the box sides to make
strong edges for tie string

Animal faces can be altered very
easily by changing ear shape and
position, and by moving the eye

Mask made from any cereal or soap
powder carton, or other available card

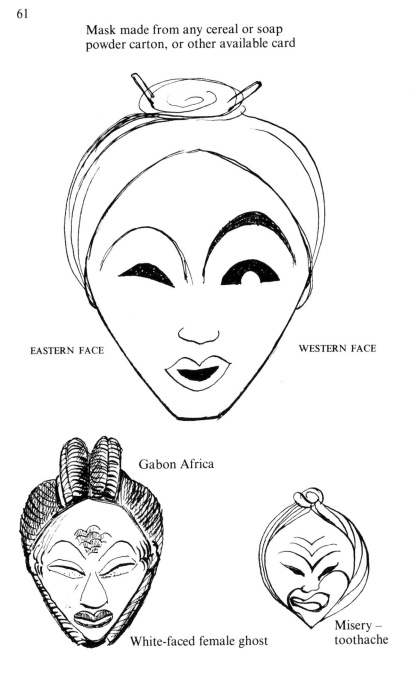

EASTERN FACE   WESTERN FACE

Gabon Africa

White-faced female ghost

Misery –
toothache

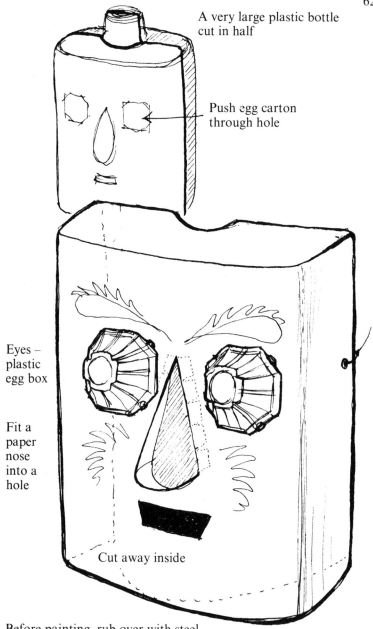

A very large plastic bottle cut in half

Push egg carton through hole

Eyes – plastic egg box

Fit a paper nose into a hole

Cut away inside

Before painting, rub over with steel wool to roughen the surface

EVIL

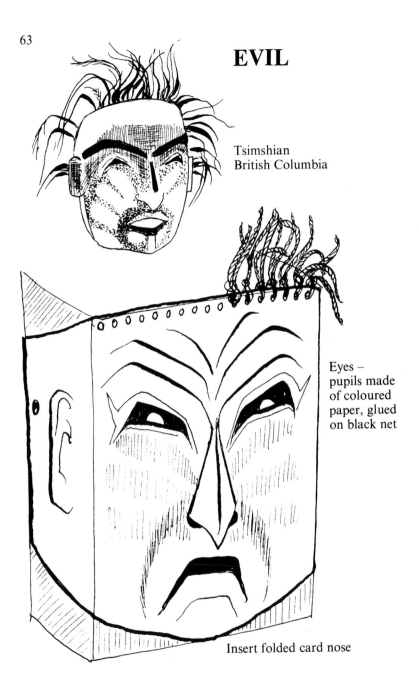

Tsimshian
British Columbia

Eyes –
pupils made
of coloured
paper, glued
on black net

Insert folded card nose

COWARD
SELF-PITY
OGRE
HEN-PECKED MAN

Ceremonial tablet
Papuan Gulf
New Guinea

Receding or protruding eyes of
plastic egg carton which look
rheumy or tearful

Painted nose or padded paper

Purple wool under eye openings

Hair – wool lightly brushed with
Marvin medium to stiffen

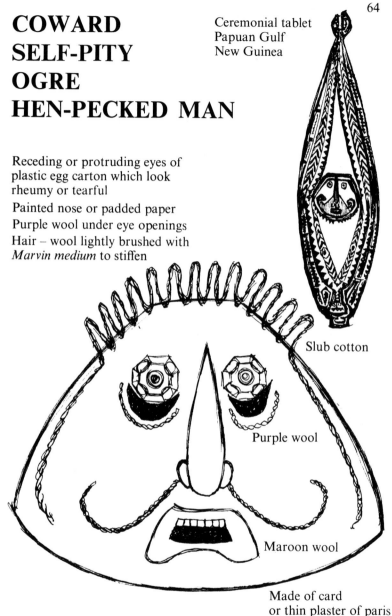

Slub cotton

Purple wool

Maroon wool

Made of card
or thin plaster of paris
or buckram

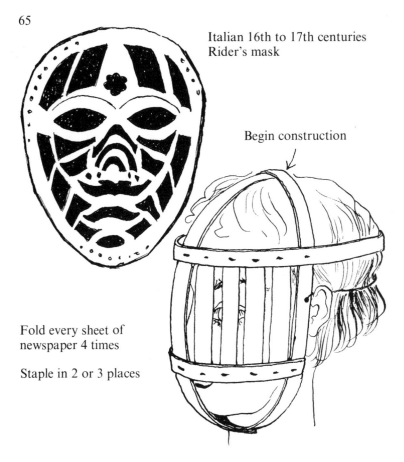

Italian 16th to 17th centuries
Rider's mask

Begin construction

Fold every sheet of
newspaper 4 times

Staple in 2 or 3 places

Make several such bands,
joining them together with
staples until long enough

Begin with the 3 long bands

Add band beneath nose, and
thin strips of paper, leaving
vision spaces between them

Secure with elastic

BALLOON MASKS

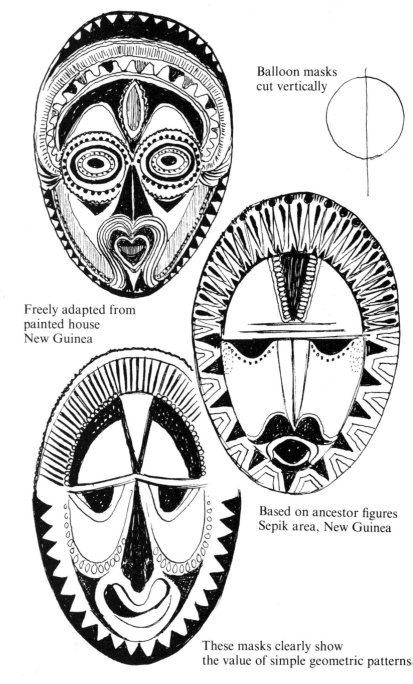

Balloon masks
cut vertically

Freely adapted from
painted house
New Guinea

Based on ancestor figures
Sepik area, New Guinea

These masks clearly show
the value of simple geometric patterns

SUN
CLOWN
SPOOK
DEMON
HALLOWE'EN
MASK

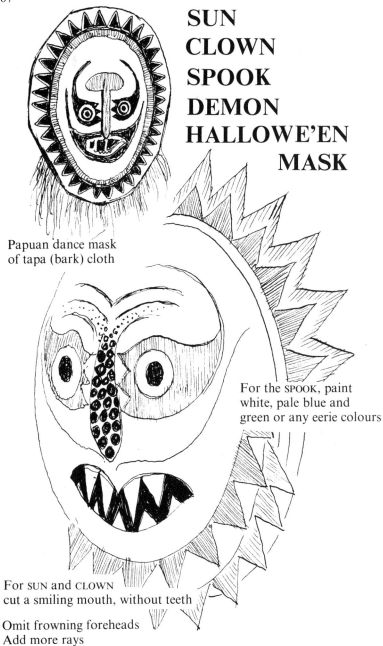

Papuan dance mask
of tapa (bark) cloth

For the SPOOK, paint
white, pale blue and
green or any eerie colours

For SUN and CLOWN
cut a smiling mouth, without teeth

Omit frowning foreheads
Add more rays

SLEEPWALKER

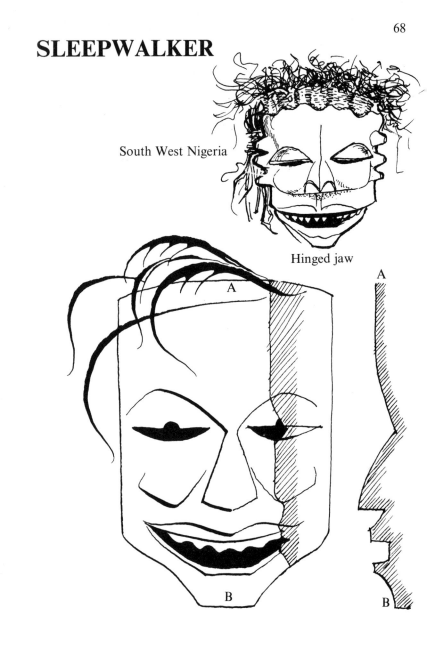

South West Nigeria

Hinged jaw

Clay mould, vaseline, muslin, thin layer of
plaster of paris, and more muslin to prevent
the plaster from shattering, if it should be
too thin

IDIOT

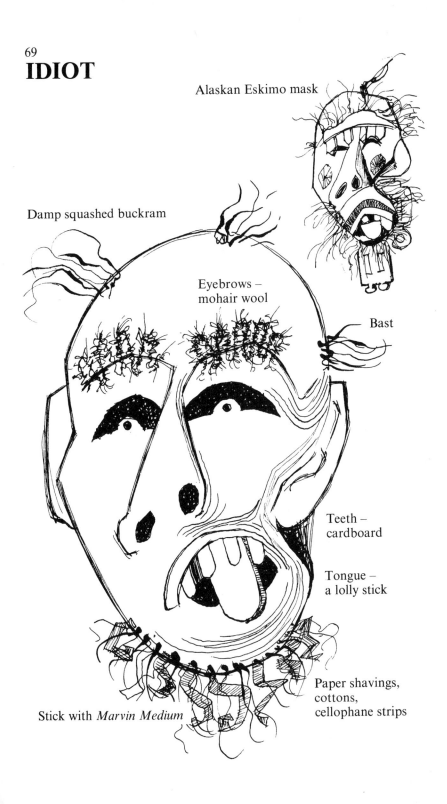

Alaskan Eskimo mask

Damp squashed buckram

Eyebrows –
mohair wool

Bast

Teeth –
cardboard

Tongue –
a lolly stick

Paper shavings,
cottons,
cellophane strips

Stick with *Marvin Medium*

Cane and tapa (bark) cloth mask
New Britain

DEMON
WITCH no spectacles

WIZARD
VERY OLD MAN
WATCHMENDER

Paint features

Old
spectacle
frames or
plastic
covered
wire, rims
glued to mask

A   B

Tie cotton
round A B while
buckram dries

Glue nose and
ears on to face
when it has set

Damp buckram,
squashed into
shape, needs a
little watchful
coaxing to prevent
it from spreading out

Fuzzy wool beard

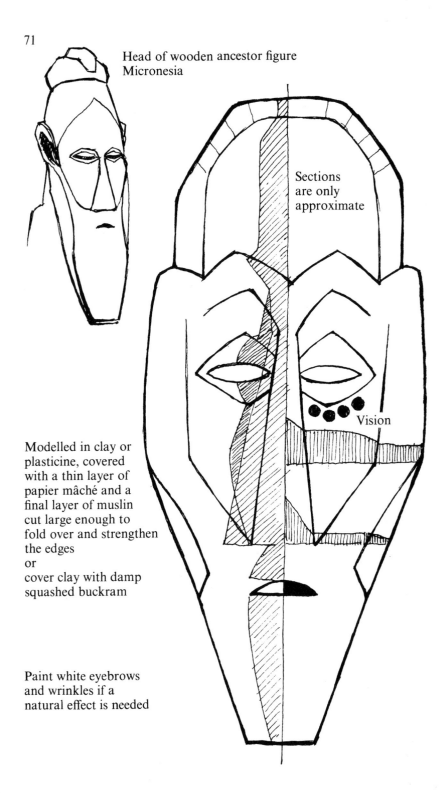

71

Head of wooden ancestor figure
Micronesia

Sections
are only
approximate

Vision

Modelled in clay or
plasticine, covered
with a thin layer of
papier mâché and a
final layer of muslin
cut large enough to
fold over and strengthen
the edges
or
cover clay with damp
squashed buckram

Paint white eyebrows
and wrinkles if a
natural effect is needed

OGRE GIANT

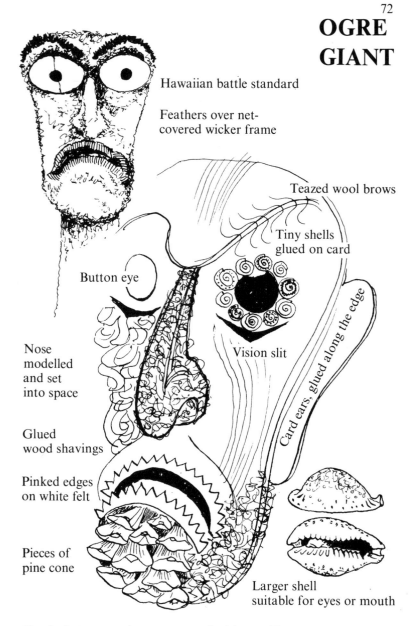

Hawaiian battle standard

Feathers over net-covered wicker frame

Teazed wool brows

Tiny shells glued on card

Button eye

Vision slit

Card ears, glued along the edge

Nose modelled and set into space

Glued wood shavings

Pinked edges on white felt

Pieces of pine cone

Larger shell suitable for eyes or mouth

Crushed corrugated paper covered with towelling into which other decoration is pressed hard and firmly glued with *Marvin medium*

Double face mask
Senufo, West Africa

The mask is wide, leaving enough space inside for the nose

Cut normal eye holes and paint the sham eyes a dark tone
to keep the effect balanced

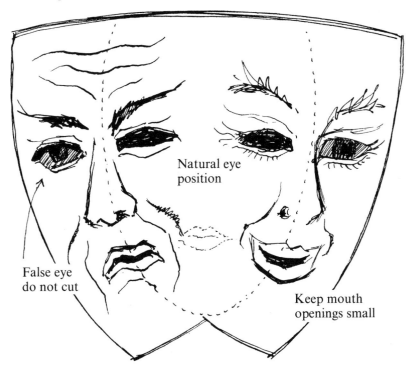

Natural eye
position

False eye
do not cut

Keep mouth
openings small

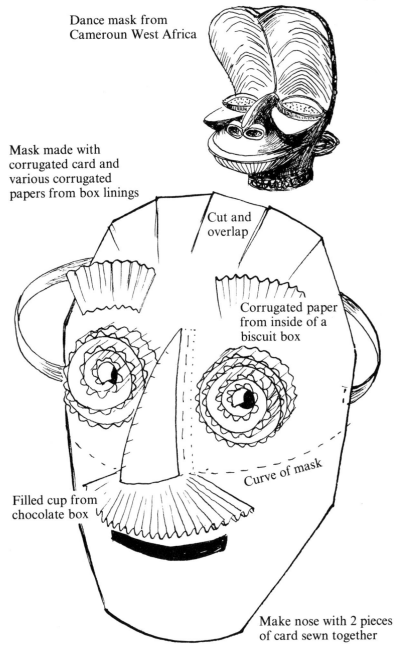

Dance mask from
Cameroun West Africa

Mask made with
corrugated card and
various corrugated
papers from box linings

Cut and
overlap

Corrugated paper
from inside of a
biscuit box

Filled cup from
chocolate box

Curve of mask

Make nose with 2 pieces
of card sewn together

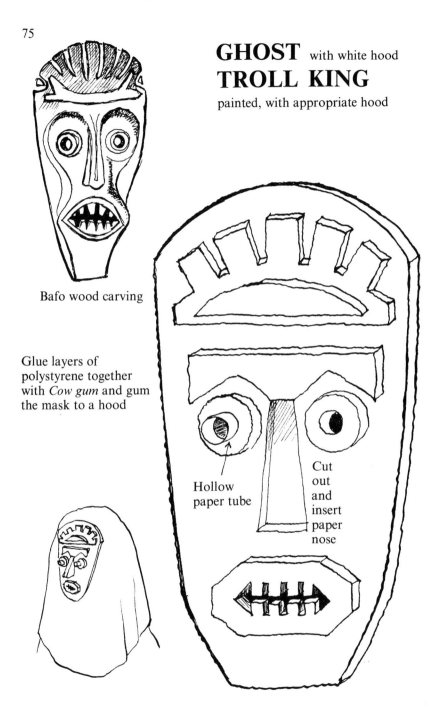

GHOST with white hood
TROLL KING
painted, with appropriate hood

Bafo wood carving

Glue layers of
polystyrene together
with *Cow gum* and gum
the mask to a hood

Hollow
paper tube

Cut
out
and
insert
paper
nose

MONKEY

suggested by Kwakiutl painted
wood mask, British Columbia

Original, off-white with pink
and smoke-grey detail

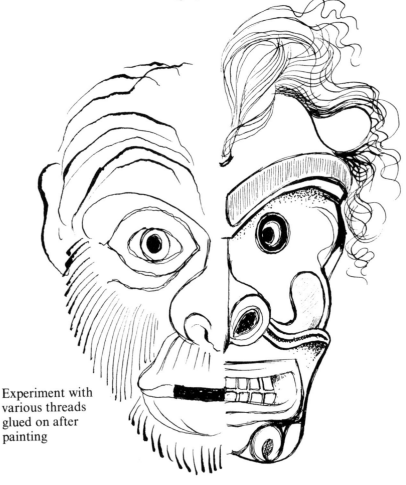

Experiment with
various threads
glued on after
painting

Animal adaptation   Kwakiutl mask

MAN PUNCH CLOWN
PARROT EAGLE

The powerful wood carving of this Bella Coola mask
can be studied to advantage before modelling in clay or
plasticine, for papier mâché. The deeply undercut
nose should not prove difficult if the 'skin' is removed
from the forehead downwards

STRAWMAN
LION from *The Wizard of Oz*

American Plains,
Indian corn-husk mask

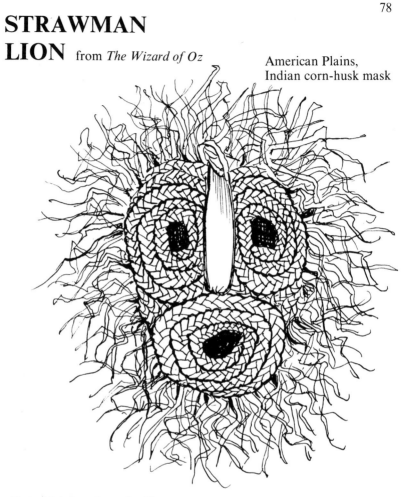

Plait thick bunches of raffia

Sew plaits together in 3 spirals, leaving
centre holes for eyes and mouth

Stuff the foot of a nylon stocking for the nose

Make the hair or mane of rope, straw and raffia
mixed with narrow strips of fabric

HAT, HELMET and HOOD MASKS

Firespitter mask
Senufo, West Africa
Ivory Coast

Hat masks which fit securely on the head, generally leave the face completely uncovered. Some massive bird masks worn in American Coastal Indian dances project far beyond the forehead, shading but not hiding the face. The loud snapping of a raven's beak makes the stylised movement and eerie music all the more dramatic. The Tlingit, from the same area, use rolling eyes and a moveable jaw controlled by string. In parts of West Africa helmet masks, worn horizontally, are attached to a hood which covers the entire body, suggesting the animal represented. Certain South Pacific helmet masks have the subject on top of the head, rather like a crest. These might be classed as headdresses were it not that their function is identical with that of a mask.

CHESS PIECES

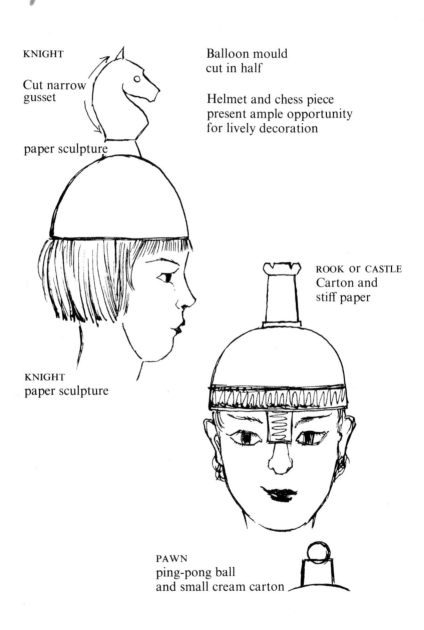

KNIGHT

Cut narrow gusset

paper sculpture

Balloon mould cut in half

Helmet and chess piece present ample opportunity for lively decoration

KNIGHT
paper sculpture

ROOK or CASTLE
Carton and stiff paper

PAWN
ping-pong ball
and small cream carton

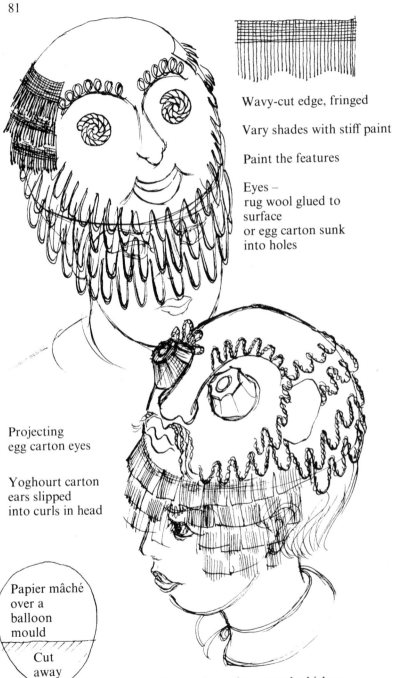

Wavy-cut edge, fringed

Vary shades with stiff paint

Paint the features

Eyes –
rug wool glued to
surface
or egg carton sunk
into holes

Projecting
egg carton eyes

Yoghourt carton
ears slipped
into curls in head

Papier mâché
over a
balloon
mould

Cut
away

Rope hair, eyebrows and whiskers

LION   HELMET MASK

Balloon base

Brown corrugated paper
ears with ridges inside

Very thick rope for
eyes and nose

HEN

Felt tongue

Thread raffia
through tape,
fold over and
either glue or
staple to mask

The ballet
La Fille Mal Gardée
begins with a dance in
which cock and hens wear
hat masks

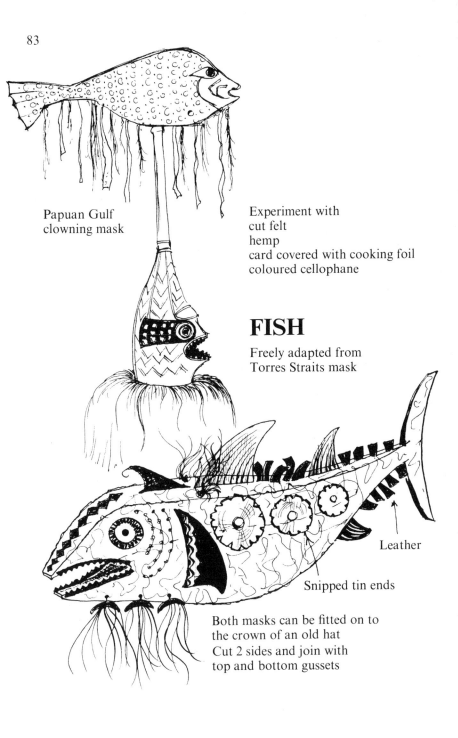

Papuan Gulf
clowning mask

Experiment with
cut felt
hemp
card covered with cooking foil
coloured cellophane

FISH

Freely adapted from
Torres Straits mask

Leather

Snipped tin ends

Both masks can be fitted on to
the crown of an old hat
Cut 2 sides and join with
top and bottom gussets

WOLF
HELMET MASK

Kwakiutl
North West Coast Indian

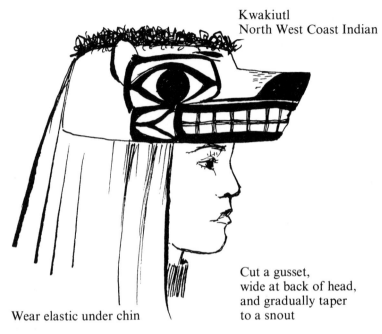

Cut a gusset,
wide at back of head,
and gradually taper
to a snout

Wear elastic under chin

Cut two side pieces and gusset
Use thin card or paper, covered with muslin

Add fur over top of head, and a hood

EAGLE HELMET MASK

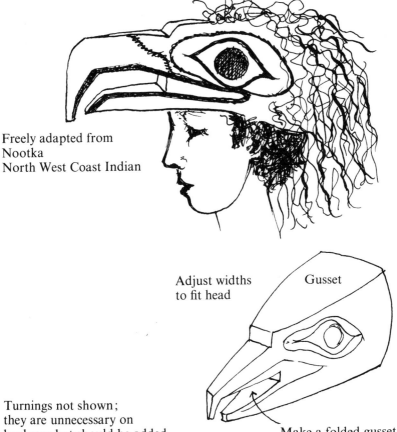

Freely adapted from
Nootka
North West Coast Indian

Adjust widths
to fit head

Gusset

Turnings not shown;
they are unnecessary on
buckram but should be added
for card or corrugated card

Make a folded gusset
for inside mouth

GROUP MASK
OCTO

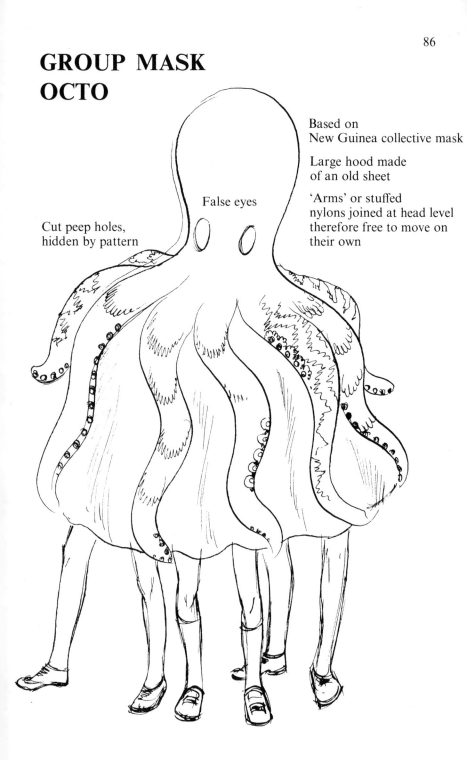

False eyes

Based on
New Guinea collective mask

Large hood made
of an old sheet

'Arms' or stuffed
nylons joined at head level
therefore free to move on
their own

Cut peep holes,
hidden by pattern

Big Heads are carnival masks about 915 mm (3 ft) high, which rest on the shoulders. While all masks tend to be over life size Big Heads, gross and entirely out of proportion, are so made to project high above crowds watching a procession.

Big Heads are awkward to balance on young shoulders and should be very light weight. They can be made of thin papier mâché or sized calico over a wire or plastic mesh frame, attached to an upturned plastic bucket, which forms the neck and conceals the true head. Vision and breathing holes must be cut in the neck and hidden by shadows in folds of a painted scarf or similar draped material. Wire ends need to be nipped close or turned in with pliers. Thin papier mâché can be strengthened with butter muslin.

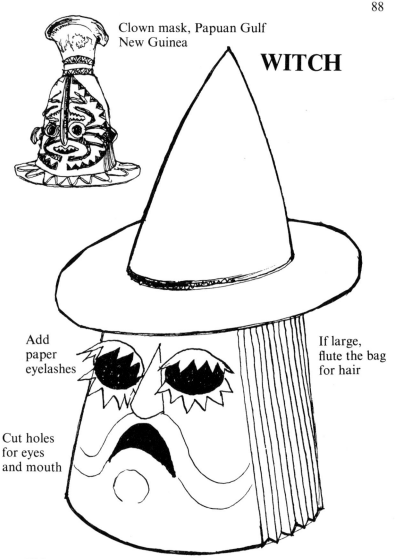

Clown mask, Papuan Gulf
New Guinea

WITCH

Add
paper
eyelashes

If large,
flute the bag
for hair

Cut holes
for eyes
and mouth

Either
use a big strong paper bag, twist and tie
the closed end, cover 'knot' with hat, and
glue where edges touch
or
begin with a cardboard cone base, adding
folded paper hair

HOOD MASK

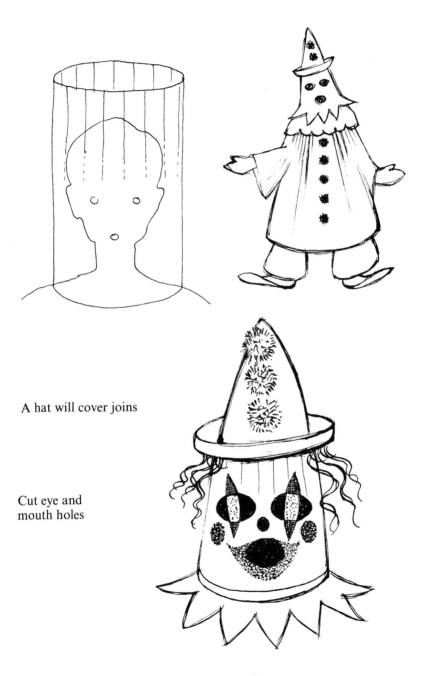

A hat will cover joins

Cut eye and
mouth holes

PAPER BAG MASK

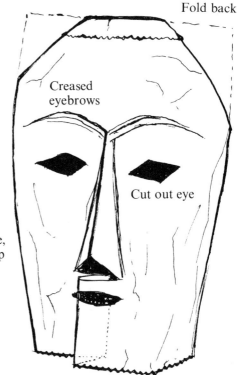

Commemorative figure
wood carving, Assam

Fold back

Creased
eyebrows

Cut out eye

Crease down
centre for a nose,
cut across the tip

Colour with
paint or crayon

Overlap, flatten and paste,
cut out the mouth

Bucket shaped masks worn by children at a
Gloucestershire Junior school while acting
an event in local history

BIBLIOGRAPHY

F BOAZ *Primitive Art* Dover Publication Inc New York

E O CHRISTENSEN *Primitive Art* Thames and Hudson London and Thomas Y Crowell Company New York

D DUERDEN *African Art* Hamlyn London

D FRASER *Primitive Art* Thames and Hudson London

J GREGOR *Masks of the World* Batsford London 1936 (out of print)

G GRIGSON *Art Treasures of the British Museum* Thames and Hudson London

J GUIART *Arts of the South Pacific* Thames and Hudson London

E LEUZINGER *Africa* Methuen London

F MONTI *African Masks* Hamlyn London

G PARRINDER *African Mythology* Hamlyn London

O RILEY *Masks and Magic* Thames and Hudson London

E ROTTGER *Creative Paper Craft* Batsford London Van Nostrand Reinhold New York

R UNDERHILL *Indians of the Pacific Northwest* US Office of Indian Affairs

BBC TALKS FOR VI FORMS   *African Art*

The Unesco Courier   October 1959, December 1965, December 1970

Traditional Sculptures from the Colonies   HMSO

Masks, the many faces of man   Exhibition catalogue, Toronto Royal Ontario Museum 1964

Descriptive booklet   Alaskan Historical Museum, Junean, Alaska

Primitive Art from Chicago collections   Art Institute of Chicago

Senufo Sculpture from West Africa   Museum of Primitive Art, New York 1963

Masks and Men Science Guide No 128   The American Museum of Natural History, New York

INDEX